Meeting Friends

Building Bridges Series

Building Bridges Series: Meeting Friends
Text by Catherine White
Illustrations by Marta Kwasniewska
Copyright © Gatehouse Media Limited 2017

First published and distributed in 2017 by Gatehouse Media Limited

ISBN: 978-1-84231-176-9

British Library Cataloguing-in-Publication Data:
A catalogue record for this book is available from the British Library

Calman Colaiste
Wisbech Road
Thorney
Peterborough
PE6 0TD

No part of this publication may be reproduced in any form or by any means, electronic, mechanical, photocopying, recording or otherwise, without the prior written consent of the publishers.

Jamal goes to the café to meet his friend, Ali.
He looks around for Ali.
Ali is not there yet,
so Jamal sits at a table near the door.
Ali will see me when he comes in, he thinks.

Jamal looks around the café.
The café is busy.

An old man and woman sit quietly.
A man is reading a newspaper.

A young mum is feeding her toddler.
A baby is asleep in the pram next to her.
A young couple are chatting and
smiling at each other.
A woman is tapping away on her laptop.

Jamal sees a girl sitting at the next table.
Jamal knows her from college.
They were on the same course last year.
Their eyes meet and Jamal smiles at her.
The girl smiles back.

Jamal says, "Hello Sara, how are you?"

"Hello Jamal, I'm very well, thanks.
It's good to see you," says Sara.

They talk about college.
They talk about their friends.
They talk about their old tutor
and the funny things he did in class.

"What are you doing now?" Jamal asks.
"Do you have a job?"

"I have a job in the health centre," Sara says.
"I work in the office. What about you?"

"I'm still at college.
I want to go to university
to study engineering," says Jamal.

Jamal tells Sara that he is waiting for Ali.
He is pleased that Ali is late.
Jamal likes Sara.
He thinks that Sara likes him, too.

"Would you like another coffee, Sara?"
Jamal asks.

"Yes, please," Sara says.
"Come and sit at my table.
We can wait for Ali together."

If you have enjoyed this book, why not try another title in the *Building Bridges Series:*

Going to College
Finding a Home
Getting a Job
Going Shopping
Seeing the Doctor

Gatehouse Books®

Gatehouse Books are written for older teenagers and adults who are developing their basic reading and writing or English language skills.

The format of our books is clear and uncluttered. The language is familiar and the text is often line-broken, so that each line ends at a natural pause.

Gatehouse Books are widely used within Adult Basic Education throughout the English speaking world. They are also a valuable resource within the Prison Education Service and Probation Services, Social Services and secondary schools - in both basic skills and ESOL teaching.

Catalogue available

Gatehouse Media Limited
PO Box 965
Warrington
WA4 9DE

Tel/Fax: 01925 267778
E-mail: info@gatehousebooks.com
Website: www.gatehousebooks.com